LETTER THAT NEVER

LETTER
THAT
NEVER

Ann Pelletier

THE WORD WORKS
WASHINGTON, D.C.

The Word Works
P.O. Box 42164
Washington, D.C. 20015
editor@wordworksbooks.org

Cover art: "Where the Blue of the Night
Meets the Cold of the Day," Laurel Jensen
Cover design: Susan Pearce Design
Author photograph: Justin Eatinger

LCCN: 2016957977
ISBN: 978-1-944585-09-9

Acknowledgments

Grateful acknowledgment to the editors of the following journals where some of these poems first appeared:

Cricket Online Review (Chad Lietz and J.D. Mitchell-Lumsden):
   "clay and mud."

New American Writing (Paul Hoover and Maxine Chernoff):
   "is it my white skull on your black beach"; ")"; "sometimes
   I would think to map the endpoint"; "I have made one
   short voyage."

New Delta Review (Danielle Lea Buchanan):
   "it was impossible" under the title "Mission."

Requited Journal (H.V. Cramond):
   "I kept those beautiful things."

Deepest gratitude to Nancy White and all the wonderful people at The Word Works. I am sustained by writing regularly with Barbara Tomash, Jesse Nissim and Nona Caspers. I am also indebted to the Ensenada Avenue poets group: Joan Baranow, Judy Halebsky, Dawn McGuire, Claudia MonPere and again, Barbara Tomash. I am indebted to my many generous and patient teachers. For their unwavering support, I am most grateful to Laurel Jensen, Susan Beale, my parents, my sister, and my brothers. Thank you, Z, R, L, S-P, and thank you, thank you, steadfast Justin.

Contents

for Claire Pelletier and Janet Pelletier

and for Justin

*She struggles with the forces that would tell her
story for her, or write her out of the story...*

—Rebecca Solnit

*I lift my head and watch the moon.
I drop my head and think of home.*

—Li Bai
(trans. Vikram Seth)

alone down the long drop I lived beneath the bridge in liquid darkness
shoulders hunched against the invisible sun

within immense shadows at the farthest edge of the valley
I lived in luck everything plentiful except for light

I would hear my mother's comfort through the haze
and sometimes my namesake

it does no good trying to preserve a sense of time and space

high wind stirred in the pines the ways of the wild
renting my sutured desire

I disembarked at night's new epicenter
dissociated and dislocated

there had been boats, swans, parks with labeled trees
canaries jouncing in jewelweed

(bouncing in the back of the truck grabbing at leaves)

in a cage, actually, cloaked to stop the singing
(which was not singing)

reassigned to reeds
and raised in the company of secretives

gone are those who know I went missing

the sun made midnight shadows of the trees risen up from the snow

zigzags of cold and heat

                    impervious birds

                        where was I bound

        to dwell in the weather

        to track the surface with facility

                      what bound me

           in that all-light

           to not lose sight

           to—not—sink

knee and foot and tooth

I have come out of dry waves
I follow the grass I accept the grace
I light my own way I create my own illusion

I am the scant known strain I am right angles
fresh fuel crude beginning merely breathing
small matter

and what perils!

each night I shift a little

compelled by a failure of momentum only do I rove nocturnally

in the mountain timber
    tender fold in the road
        over the systole of the sea

        thick-growing violets   disciples of camouflage

            the way is not—

        (despite deep evidence)   (evidence of absence)

                                —I am not unfindable

silver chorus of the chain link fence

                                verging on too late
                                a day is coming when
                                this day won't be remembered

a family voice I had forgotten *oh dear oh dear oh dear*

I now know no one—will this be my final home—working alone

tink tink of sharp snow against a window and the sound of lost leaves
words falling away and words obliterated and without saying goodbye
adios blindfold bird words in lowly movement linking word to word

will no one enjoy the refrain of my rustling

I would be the bird eating three times its weight
in crickets and worms and as with the Cooper's hawk
a warbler at the feeder

I am sorry

                    no reply no reply

      I will not be revealing the nature of the crime
      for which our people stand accused

      pick something you couldn't bear
      were it true

                    no reply no reply

to watch and to not watch at the same time

              at what point does the wriggling warbler die

      when did doubt become our absolute

there are all sorts of Edens from which one can be flung
making Eden moot

which bright ill might reveal

                      a little hidden sympathy

          what nocturnal offerings

                            the gods are tense and terse
                              perched in the place
                                  I am forbidden to travel

         (why have this voice if not
          to speak)
                   (why these eyes)

                                 why try to deceive me

there will be no calling of my witnesses

                            come morning

          no innocence / no denying

what would it be like to live
according to the gods of luck

        rabbit running for the dun glimmer

what remains of
           the touch I relished
           the future's distance

        the cat   the fiddle

        my days are passed in thirst / hunger

what would it be like to find
the promised philtre

what—*what* is *necessary*
               to apprehend

before my blouses had been unbuttoned
before I bore this distinctive name
before the establishment of this new style

before crossing the fraying bridge (or shortly thereafter)
before restrictions and closures
before being chased by the bird faking wing break

how was I to proceed?

before natural forces
before allowing anyone to
before shaking these silver dollar petals

I would sit in my sunny doorway
marvelously lucky and naive

I was once alive   only just arrived

I would pass the season   in surpassing love

the most delicious things   held out to me

suggestion of stars   in a dark green sky

weed seeds   blowing in a random wind

that evolution before   the end begins

)

I would be watching a bird of ochre flank code a hole in a living tree

a private method and it returns   (nothing

please wait   I *will* open this concrete place

      a cone dropping from somewhere above and the black and white
      birds retch and trade branches

(false void)   (nothing to do with

      (false voice) tick of the executioners sequestered in the chaparral
           (hooded) (plump as friars)

                    please wait one moment more

     boulders all around and the ground ground-up granite
     the wind sweeps in with a whiff of shit shifting the season
     now would be the days for the meat-eating bees

I closed the book
I made a mattress out of duff
I opened the door for the animal
I circled
where is the place on the helix for temptation?
what is the mutation for tribulation?
all the branches were taken by talkative finches leaving
no place to perch in peace
I was asked if I enjoy making the innocent suffer
and I thought what I enjoy is ice cream and I thought maple walnut
and I thought of the shack on Route 4
and I thought suffer? innocent?
and I thought of my father in the house he built
and I thought scissor truss and I thought stress-skin panel
and I thought of my father hoisting those beams
and I think of him now with the last stair built
spending his evenings weeping over the singers on his tv
there is so little time
shall I take his hammer to the captain
shall I be a dandy shall I be a rover
would he know who I am by the songs that I sing
where is the locus for the harm we inflict
where are the words I apologize
I planned my last meal

was I yet alive   in some mode still unknown   typically depicted

with cat   worshiped heretofore   meeting a lover at the bridge

setting a pattern for suffering   implying my moral imperative

pry open this mouth   of foolish opinion   transformed into any

possible shape   the corollary   fallen into this *can never get out*

presumed   subsumed   bemused   left at that   never before

attempted in this age   contending by some inevitable cause

scattered abroad   elsewhere signified   worthy of my difficulty

all in all   outlawed   at ease   able to drink poison   standing

laudably   cured   carting a pile of rocks   holding an open book

slaying an agony   in no need of my name   still in my mourning

sleep   protected by vultures   ready and at hand   spent and gone half-sighted

I live in lunar lure

ambivalent & polymorphous

shaped by not the least signal

dim circumference of a single window

what *is* living color

I subsist on light I hoard

this little body   goes rising

this body flies   and croaking cries

needing, needling   blind birthed body

to the woods   wends the body

branch by branch   the body guided

potent   latent   lustered   long-wanting

this body rallies to fables   re: the course of its ravenings

crusted and clawed   this body's song

sometimes I think to map the endpoint: where x turns y

    all day long
    this silver sky

    stamped coin
    dainty dish

how easy to alter one's promise (premise) (x // y)

    all day long this
    battered box

    icon of fright

sometimes I think to will the power and nature of spirits

    sunlight
    penetrates

    seems to change my life

    knife knife
    knife

    (almost) (not quite)

I close my eyes and say why I'm here / on this island
on the anniversary of my crime

I have gone to the hole where unexpected things might happen
then don't and don't / for fifty years / wresting

        to be redeemed
        (but who can say this aloud?)
        an error so wide—

we rarely mention our mothers / many times we have asked:
who is my father?

I devoured my hosts and so deprived myself of a home

yet to see the unbelieved-in (goodness) in me
the unbelieved-in simple scheme

        starlings on the loops of wire / calm and nervous
        I know who I am / elemental spirit
        like the coyote in snow / I take small steps walk a straight line

the forged forgiveness does not seem to be enough / recast my role
I turn myself in

fathoms from the truth
farthest from the seed of light

running cold water
cooling old stars

I am all alone now
waiting for orders

winter green in the bottom sky

is there still warmth
unlock the little door

I should answer the question
what happened to me
I should reach
sometimes no one
a bent body
no body
a reservoir
how do I cross over
how do I love my neighbor
sometimes desire rises
like bile
when do I know I am not in danger
can no one order the world
(no)
sometimes a voice within my voice
whatever is a moment
sometimes a moment

there were puddles in the road and trees turning
into people who might not leave alive

and each time I glanced back it was
perhaps the last time

do you know what you ask?

trees dying at the top of the hill
and the subtle winter birds
solitary in impermanent colonies

being in charge of someone's life
—lives measured in seconds—
is not the same as love

let us never speak

long white neck
long black legs

who can *learn* abstinence

have I been led astray

I have been in and out
of deserts

terrible claws
terrifying breathing beast

I have been
unpleasant

white bowls brimmed with
figs, lemons

what might it mean to live
according to nature

I have been one of two killers
competing for adoration

can instinct cleave from reason

where am I now?
why, hiding from my own approach

lured by light
    back into the night

mist & small rain

last   wishing   late
is it not possible to wholly disinhabit

locked gate

I asked some questions
    here & there

(I was told to wait)

my double wings were pinched from poppy sleep

                              my double wings

drifting to snag like trash
                              in a sycamore

what is the color of

      this clear sky I see with my own eyes

blue heron at dusk / dusk itself

      mother tongue

here is a letter with a line drawing of the prison and its prisoner

      naked is the color of certain rocks

            icy spring / the peril of its current

distillation under the surface—the fracturing of every thought

         into what pure word

     how long was that time of

        waiting to breathe

the sun to reach the meridian

       how far was that distance from the beginning

perfidy   burning

              around me   tinted sound

       epilobium

tyger-lily   a new vision

     pox   (I wish I could stop)

        naked   land

      feet   locked

self-forced pacing

inflected with the rhythm of replicated infirmity

                open woods

                   or

                forest openings

   smite

slit   these were the dark days of trial

     seize

                dress

    take away my voice   undress

                duress

from every window

where is the fix of the faint south star

inclement days long I lay looking up through the skylight
discovering rare milk-making clouds

I was said to be brave
in the face

I was said to [   ]

blind when I die and buried in a rented grave
bodily remains to be evicted after five years

where? where?

I was abundantly loved
unto solitude

I was a miner trudging to the shaft

dimly visible was my danger along a path along a hedge of thorns

moods of mere endurance alternating with a violence of abundance

      ·

how was it to live that life
                tamping morning snow

I don't remember   anyone's names

I remember invoking   Saint Joseph

I don't remember the last time   I swept

I remember a summer   polyphony

fish   baked in a covered dish

I can't remember   the clustering bees

I do remember   perfect stillness   then the tree falling

where I'd only just passed   as in a dream

the valley   looking back   my father

I remember morning   and being very near to love

knowing   what I could not know

how neither my eyes nor my mouth   would open

I misremember   invoking

I don't remember   my saints

I have forgotten   what is after this life

along with the version   I liked

was I aware of the shapes surrounding me?
I became a place of
                    quiet   remove

                    .

what animated my interior?
that I was alcove   primary   that I was over \ under

                    .

how did I create this longed-for?

                    .

I was climbing up into a tree house

                    .

secluded I was   steep

                    .

didn't I come closer?

                    .

here are my layers of information
as seen in the photo above

was I not configured typically?

                    .

sliding   screened

how am I like the lid of a box?
wait-and-see

it was impossible
baby boys belonging to the tall woman
impossible
a watermelon
impossibly large as a piebald ox
the gold of light
impossible that I was me
missing notes as in old piano
impossible virtue
the sweets of life
the fruit of the poor lemon
a solo show in London
a religion of the art of life
impossible to carry on so disastrously
impossible inroad
comprehension preservation acquisition
grace to the soul
impossible
wearing clothes
clouds
concrete

thus was I to return to the wake of the earth

hair combed / face washed

with a wish to give

what I loved best

without begetting

make me want to stay beyond the green door

make me a nestlike suggestion

make me want to journey here alone

make me want

make me a fantastic future

near the wild animals

this darkness is my world

make me arpeggiated

make me a pocket of space

how this night continues

make me sing of unseen hosts

make me all eyes make me ever and

make me sparingly

make me safety

make me new or renewed

is it my white skull on your black beach

bad ass   zero-hundred hours   only a narrow strip

was I disappeared
           into the populace

how to say thank you how to say please

      did I wrestle

          sometimes the soul gets away

please convey these bones to cloud street

          sometimes the core goes awry

o for the world as whole—not a fact *about* the world

      oranges and olives
             pock pock

o for the world as kempt / swept

nightjar calling—owl calling
caught in the worthless glow

who will hear this story told

this last lap in the boat
this work that will go unsigned

such hush
cradled keel

where are they
to whom I might flee

every day I am in the twilight of mood / every day I am tidings
I exaggerate the illusion / I rectify the ratio

I carry the scar of failing to clear the trees / I carry the scare of vice versa

I wander from w to w / I am to look for a place to—
I turn and face the lee

see you later sings the sparrow

I think back to the nothingness preceded by the swarming
I came here to live as long as I live / I have thus far digressed

wake up

I probe the mud for warmth / *thou shalt*

frequently I am mistaken

nothing save— / I have heard of one that— / it is not so with me

daily I played in the gaze
    of the statue of the fallen angel

whose shadow would creep steadily
    under the hidden sun

the trouble has always been
    arousing hope

if this belief would not creep

if this faith would stay in place

the trouble has been
    the blackened sky

migraines
    mania

death of the mother
    inadequate friends

if the ice would close in

if in the fields the flowers would go to seed

if chipped wing the angel
    come with me now

on the other side of the door
a squirrel shook his tambourine

loo loo skip to my loo

in lieu of prayer
each day began with a wish

ambushed with beauty
I lived in false spring

(fat-bodied—my hours—
secret & solo—inessential)

one colt-like splotch of light standing over
a hunch of snow before reeling up & away

thickening mist   afterglow   two blue heralds

I received intermittent gifts

black spot in the meadow

I retreated into the most readily available
of the opposing poles

ought I not to be

a burst of gold

what can free me from this chastisement

let me hear from you

the span of human life
must include ugliness

must red flowers in a green field

the hills and the stars and the waters / too I had a kind of
blindness / arrows
    pointing up / and the
    silhouette commanding
        turn around

   this sod would be for feet the road for wheels the steeps
   consigned to four-legged animals / trees
   leaned / arrows pointed
       down / sharp bark
        exploding

      revolution!
     surrender...

moonlight smudged by the lumpy land / and people
only pretending what they seem to know

empty space is what I sought

                    noiseless and possible

                              all snow below

days get louder (as the obscured ovenbird calling   calling)

where is the source? what is the source? how did I come to rest here?
        three stropped stakes

everywhere I've ever traveled sere birds circle / peck
        red rock white rock sidewalk   caw caw

              make it stop

yes it came to pass that I would tantrum and I would fuss and I would woun
and I would be removed to a space of lawful solitude
divested of my interior crimes and tender self-incrimination

                    now I've trod on what I wanted
                    null space gone

I kept those beautiful things   glass slats

I fenced myself   I, narrow   I, scattered with stones

I, a spine   a vertical caterpillar

I, monopolizing   testing my powers in action

not in vain   I, vain   a long view to the ocean

I, actually composed of small—

of farewells and explosives

I, a solid wall house   outside rather than in

I, an already old   done with sentiment

I kept those things

I kept those beautiful things for their own good

I kept those things to set me light

foolish to me now this fraud of the song cycle
this last of its kind this essential ceremony

take offer thank you please

silver slivers of spurned belief
all my pretty words submerged in silty creeks

follow all the rules

whose advice sits astride?

burro landscape (volcanic / glacial)
feet climb their exile (rhythm largo)

what was best?
(windows, windows)(windows that opened with cranks)

I have made one short voyage

forging no sound at all

airy anger instead of fists and spitting

fangs

I am entirely imaginary

I am too naive for erotic charity

I am prone to disembowel magnanimity

as rue or bane or grassland grass is how I wish to live

(long ago or ages hence) (dragged or drugged or dropped)
here is where I would come to live

leaving behind—looking for a hiding place—disarmed—faltering
failing to clear the tips of the trees

                                        —tunes and voices tumbling
—crying and chanting

then a lee and the sea unrolling quiet moments (blue showing through)

                        .

shall I begin anew with swallows swooping over shadows

                        .

                                —to be alive—still—

so much takes place on a clear day
old trees bearing plum and pear and apple

clay and mud   feathers   grass stems   leaf stems   frags of coal   pcs of ston

I have considered all I have
                    every possible perspective
                                color or animal coming in wave
                    as afternoon merges lacelike
                    darkstained

every surface a different angle
                wildly the birds flying with kinked wings
                        inky gleaming white

no serious foe appearing in my own image

no ships sail by the mountains

simple leaves in the stream

all my strength to stay

for such this long time

all my strength laid on the floor

my real name =

what I've been wishing for

nothing has happened

what I was wishing for

bouquets of flowers

I shall sleep now

how much happier should I be

over stepping stones I walked lost in distance
across the downsloping stream

I was still alive
shadowed by a figure flying away from hindrances

the two trees of my destination had become a single twisted cedar listing
in the bedrock that had somehow once been molten

the sun shone while it rained
I sat and watched the hard world look soft

Notes

It was after reading Francisco Goldman's "Children of the Dirty War" (*The New Yorker*, March 19, 2012) about "los desaparecidos" of Argentina that these imagined autobiographies found their form.

Much of the poem beginning "I close my eyes and say why I'm here / on this island" quotes and misquotes the prisoners in the documentary film "Shakespeare Behind Bars," written and directed by Hank Rogerson and produced by Jilann Spitzmiller.

The poem beginning "half-sighted" borrows lines from Emily Dickinson's poems beginning "We met as Sparks—Diverging Flints," "Pain expands the time," and "Wert Thou but ill— that I might show thee."

In the poem beginning "lured by light," the phrase "small rain" is from Barbara Guest's "June."

I also took inspiration from daydreamily perusing MFK Fisher, *The Gastronomical Me*; Janet Frame, *An Autobiography*; Juan Ramon Jimenez, *Platero y Yo*; Robert S. Lemmon, *Our Amazing Birds*; Phillipa Nicolson, ed., *V. Sackville-West's Garden Book*; Donald Culross Peattie, *An Almanac for Moderns*; Samuel Pepys, *The Diary of Samuel Pepys*; Francine Prose, *The Lives of the Muses: Nine Women & the Artists They Inspired*; Leonard Shlain, *Art & Physics: Parallel Visions in Space, Time & Light*; Irving Stone and Jean Stone, eds., *Dear Theo: The Autobiography of Vincent Van Gogh*; Sarah Susanka, *Home by Design: Transforming Your House into Home*; Edwin Way Teale, *Journey into Summer*; Alexander Theroux, *The Primary Colors: Three Essays*; Sun Tzu (trans. Thomas Cleary), *The Art of War*; Stephen Whitney, *A Sierra Club Naturalist's Guide to the Sierra Nevada*.

About the Author

Ann Pelletier was raised in upstate New York; Madrid, Spain; and New Hampshire. She received her MFA in Creative Writing from San Francisco State University. Her poems have appeared in *The Antioch Review*, *New American Writing*, *Volt*, and elsewhere. She currently divides her time between Lake Tahoe and Santa Cruz, California.

About the Artist

Laurel Jensen received her MA in Creative Writing from San Francisco State University where she unexpectedly became interested in photography. Her latest project, *Walk with Me*, is a photographic journal of her encounters walking along local coastal paths. With engaging images and thought-provoking quotations, she shares her very particular eye and her love of language.

OTHER WORD WORKS BOOKS

Annik Adey-Babinski, *Okay Cool No Smoking Love Pony*
Karren L. Alenier, *Wandering on the Outside*
Karren L. Alenier, ed., *Whose Woods These Are*
Karren L. Alenier & Miles David Moore, eds.,
Winners: A Retrospective of the Washington Prize
Christopher Bursk, ed., *Cool Fire*
Barbara Goldberg, *Berta Broadfoot and Pepin the Short*
Frannie Lindsay, *If Mercy*
Elaine Magarrell, *The Madness of Chefs*
Marilyn McCabe, *Glass Factory*
Ann Pelletier, *Letter That Never*
Ayaz Pirani, *Happy You Are Here*
W. T. Pfefferle, *My Coolest Shirt*
Jacklyn Potter, Dwaine Rieves, Gary Stein, eds.,
Cabin Fever: Poets at Joaquin Miller's Cabin
Robert Sargent, *Aspects of a Southern Story*
& *A Woman from Memphis*
Fritz Ward, *Tsunami Diorama*
Amber West, *Hen & God*
Nancy White, ed., *Word for Word*

THE TENTH GATE PRIZE

Jennifer Barber, *Works on Paper*, 2015
Roger Sedarat, *Haji as Puppet*, 2016
Lisa Sewell, *Impossible Object*, 2014

THE WASHINGTON PRIZE

Nathalie Anderson, *Following Fred Astaire*, 1998
Michael Atkinson, *One Hundred Children Waiting for a Train*, 2001
Molly Bashaw, *The Whole Field Still Moving Inside It*, 2013
Carrie Bennett, *biography of water*, 2004
Peter Blair, *Last Heat*, 1999
John Bradley, *Love-in-Idleness: The Poetry of Roberto Zingarello*,
1995, 2nd edition 2014
Christopher Bursk, *The Way Water Rubs Stone*, 1988
Richard Carr, *Ace*, 2008
Jamison Crabtree, *Rel[AM]ent*, 2014
Jessica Cuello, *Hunt*, 2016
B. K. Fischer, *St. Rage's Vault*, 2012
Linda Lee Harper, *Toward Desire*, 1995
Ann Rae Jonas, *A Diamond Is Hard But Not Tough*, 1997
Frannie Lindsay, *Mayweed*, 2009
Richard Lyons, *Fleur Carnivore*, 2005
Elaine Magarrell, *Blameless Lives*, 1991, 2nd edition 2016
Fred Marchant, *Tipping Point*, 1993, 2nd edition 2013
Ron Mohring, *Survivable World*, 2003
Barbara Moore, *Farewell to the Body*, 1990
Brad Richard, *Motion Studies*, 2010
Jay Rogoff, *The Cutoff*, 1994
Prartho Sereno, *Call from Paris*, 2007, 2nd edition 2013
Enid Shomer, *Stalking the Florida Panther*, 1987
John Surowiecki, *The Hat City After Men Stopped Wearing Hats*, 2006
Miles Waggener, *Phoenix Suites*, 2002
Charlotte Warren, *Gandhi's Lap*, 2000
Mike White, *How to Make a Bird with Two Hands*, 2011
Nancy White, *Sun, Moon, Salt*, 1992, 2nd edition 2010
George Young, *Spinoza's Mouse*, 1996

THE HILARY THAM CAPITAL COLLECTION

Nathalie Anderson, *Stain*
Mel Belin, *Flesh That Was Chrysalis*
Carrie Bennett, *The Land Is a Painted Thing*
Doris Brody, *Judging the Distance*
Sarah Browning, *Whiskey in the Garden of Eden*
Grace Cavalieri, *Pinecrest Rest Haven*
Cheryl Clarke, *By My Precise Haircut*
Christopher Conlon, *Gilbert and Garbo in Love*
& *Mary Falls: Requiem for Mrs. Surratt*
Donna Denizé, *Broken like Job*
W. Perry Epes, *Nothing Happened*
David Eye, *Seed*
Bernadette Geyer, *The Scabbard of Her Throat*
Barbara G. S. Hagerty, *Twinzilla*
James Hopkins, *Eight Pale Women*
Brandon Johnson, *Love's Skin*
Marilyn McCabe, *Perpetual Motion*
Judith McCombs, *The Habit of Fire*
James McEwen, *Snake Country*
Miles David Moore, *The Bears of Paris*
& *Rollercoaster*
Kathi Morrison-Taylor, *By the Nest*
Tera Vale Ragan, *Reading the Ground*
Michael Shaffner, *The Good Opinion of Squirrels*
Maria Terrone, *The Bodies We Were Loaned*
Hilary Tham, *Bad Names for Women*
& *Counting*
Barbara Louise Ungar, *Charlotte Brontë, You Ruined My Life*
& *Immortal Medusa*
Jonathan Vaile, *Blue Cowboy*
Rosemary Winslow, *Green Bodies*
Michele Wolf, *Immersion*
Joe Zealberg, *Covalence*

INTERNATIONAL EDITIONS BOOKS

Kajal Ahmad (Alana Marie Levinson-LaBrosse, Mewan Nahro
Said Sofi, and Darya Abdul-Karim Ali Najin, trans.,
with Barbara Goldberg), *Handful of Salt*
Keyne Cheshire (trans.), *Murder at Jagged Rock: A Tragedy by Sophocles*
Jean Cocteau (Mary-Sherman Willis, trans.), *Grace Notes*
Yoko Danno & James C. Hopkins, *The Blue Door*
Moshe Dor, Barbara Goldberg, Giora Leshem, eds.,
The Stones Remember: Native Israeli Poets
Moshe Dor (Barbara Goldberg, trans.), *Scorched by the Sun*
Lee Sang (Myong-Hee Kim, trans.), *Crow's Eye View:
The Infamy of Lee Sang, Korean Poet*
Vladimir Levchev (Henry Taylor, trans.),
Black Book of the Endangered Species